S0-FPG-704

A Special Gift

for:

....

from:

....

date:

....

Illustration Copyright © 2001 Sue Lipkin

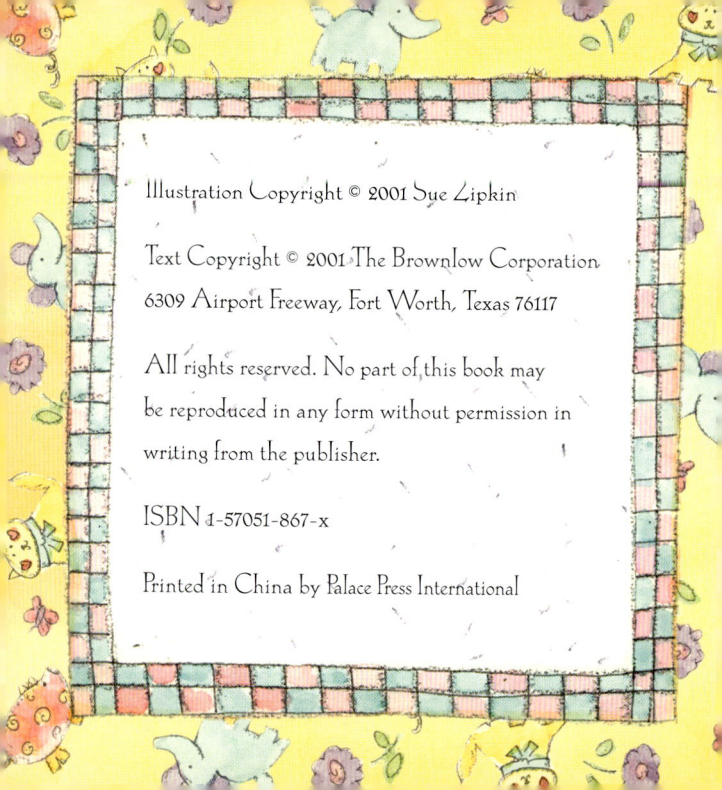

Text Copyright © 2001 The Brownlow Corporation
6309 Airport Freeway, Fort Worth, Texas 76117

All rights reserved. No part of this book may be reproduced in any form without permission in writing from the publisher.

ISBN 1-57051-867-x

Printed in China by Palace Press International

Baby Love

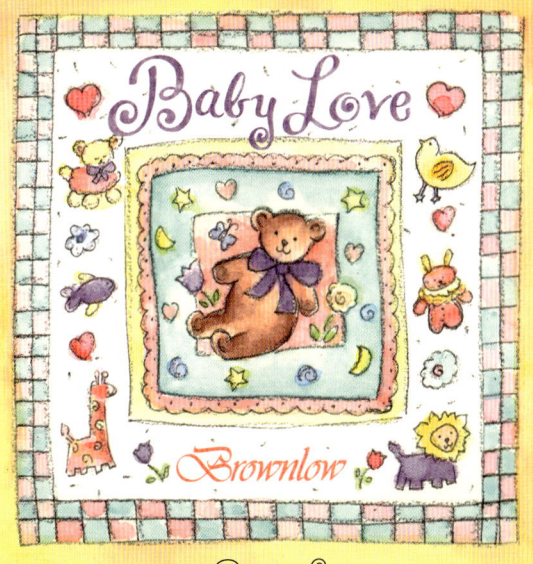

Brownlow

Edited by Rhonda S. Hogan

Illustrated by Sue Zipkin

Little Treasures Miniature Books

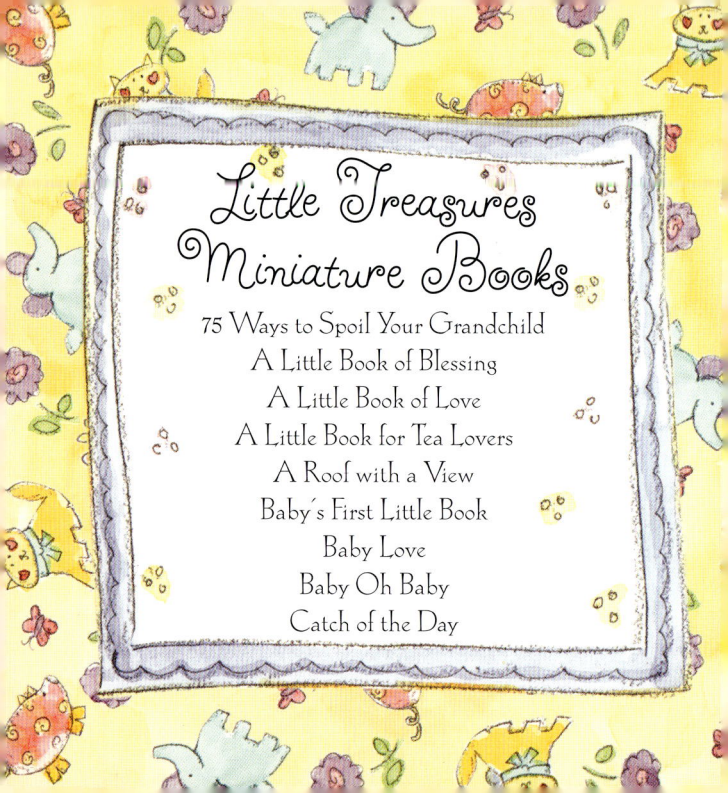

75 Ways to Spoil Your Grandchild
A Little Book of Blessing
A Little Book of Love
A Little Book for Tea Lovers
A Roof with a View
Baby's First Little Book
Baby Love
Baby Oh Baby
Catch of the Day

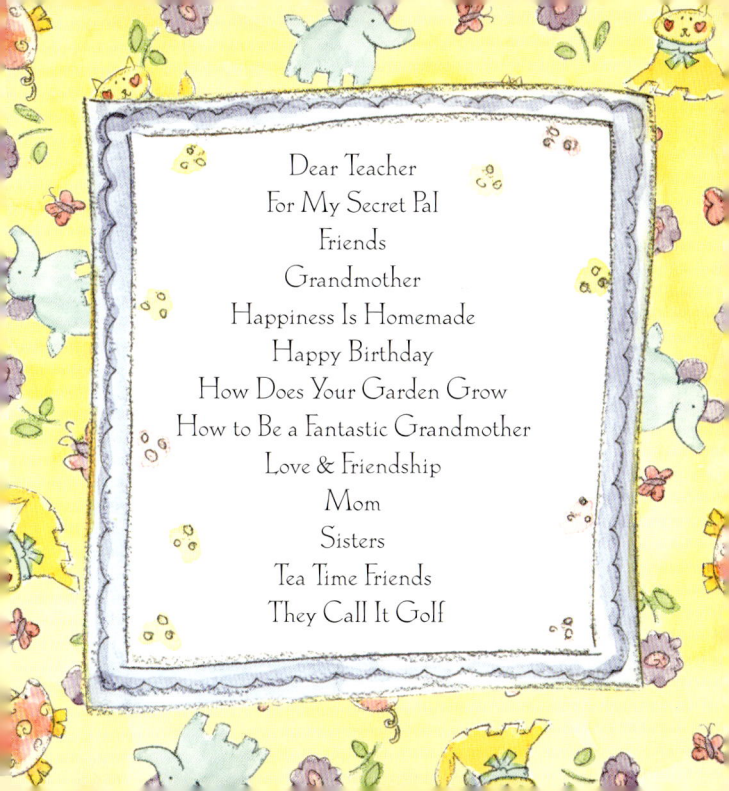

Dear Teacher
For My Secret Pal
Friends
Grandmother
Happiness Is Homemade
Happy Birthday
How Does Your Garden Grow
How to Be a Fantastic Grandmother
Love & Friendship
Mom
Sisters
Tea Time Friends
They Call It Golf

Baby Dear

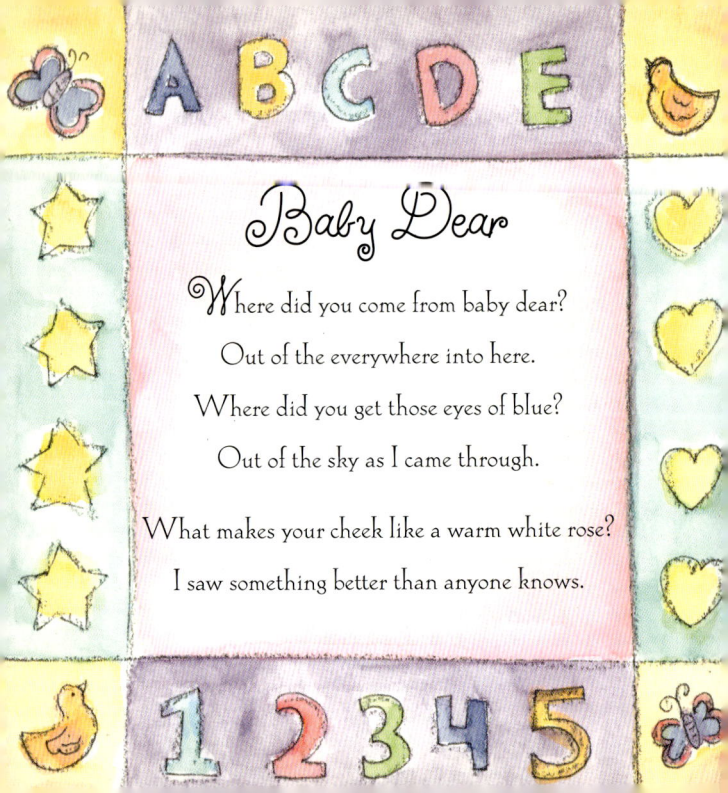

Where did you come from baby dear?

Out of the everywhere into here.

Where did you get those eyes of blue?

Out of the sky as I came through.

What makes your cheek like a warm white rose?

I saw something better than anyone knows.

Where did you get this pearly ear?

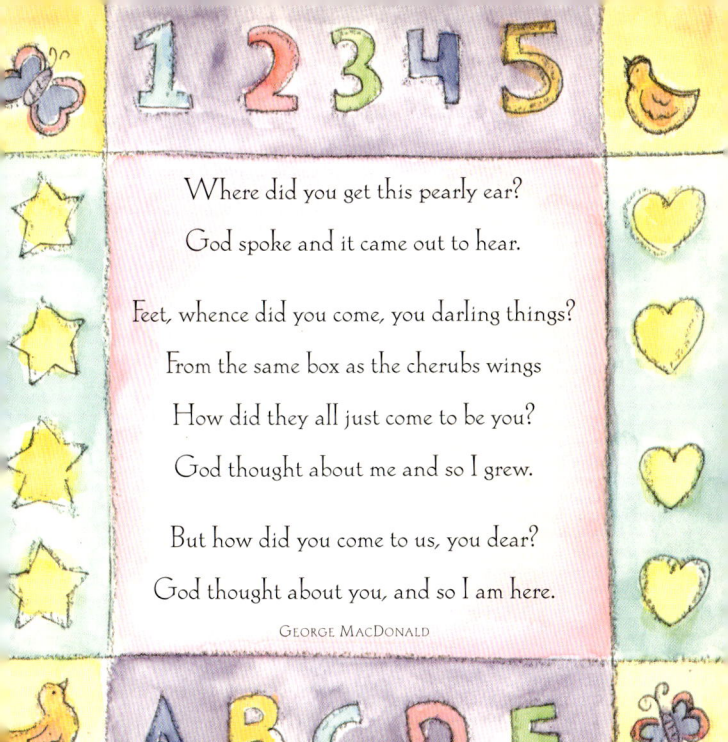

God spoke and it came out to hear.

Feet, whence did you come, you darling things?

From the same box as the cherubs wings

How did they all just come to be you?

God thought about me and so I grew.

But how did you come to us, you dear?

God thought about you, and so I am here.

GEORGE MACDONALD

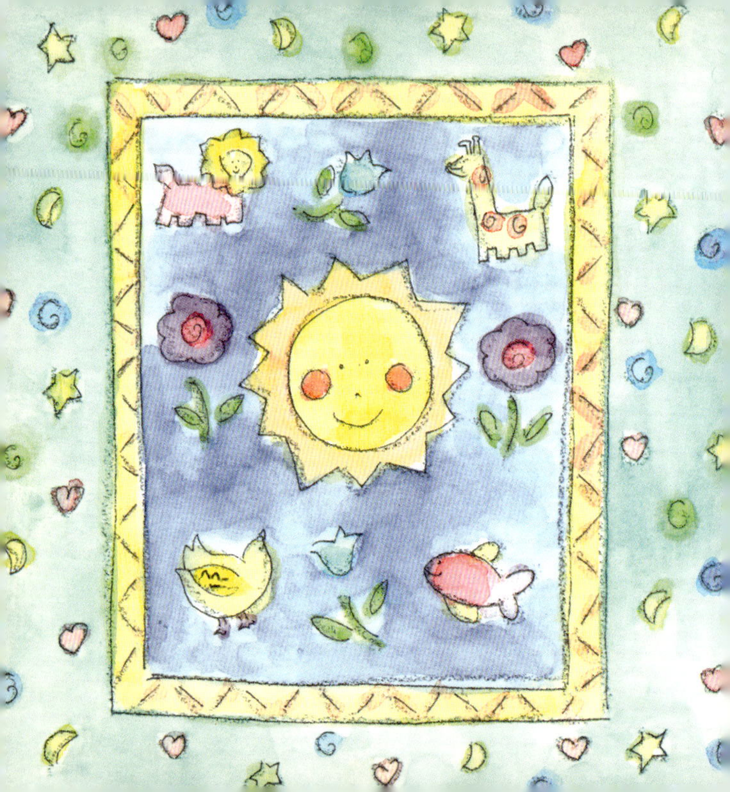

Children are a gift from the Lord.

PSALM 127:3

Every baby comes with the message that God is not yet discouraged.

RABINDRANATH TAGORE

I love these little people; and it is not a slight thing, when they, who are so fresh from God, love us.

CHARLES DICKENS

All things bright and beautiful,

All creatures great and small,

All things wise and wonderful,

The Lord God made them all.

CECIL F. ALEXANDER

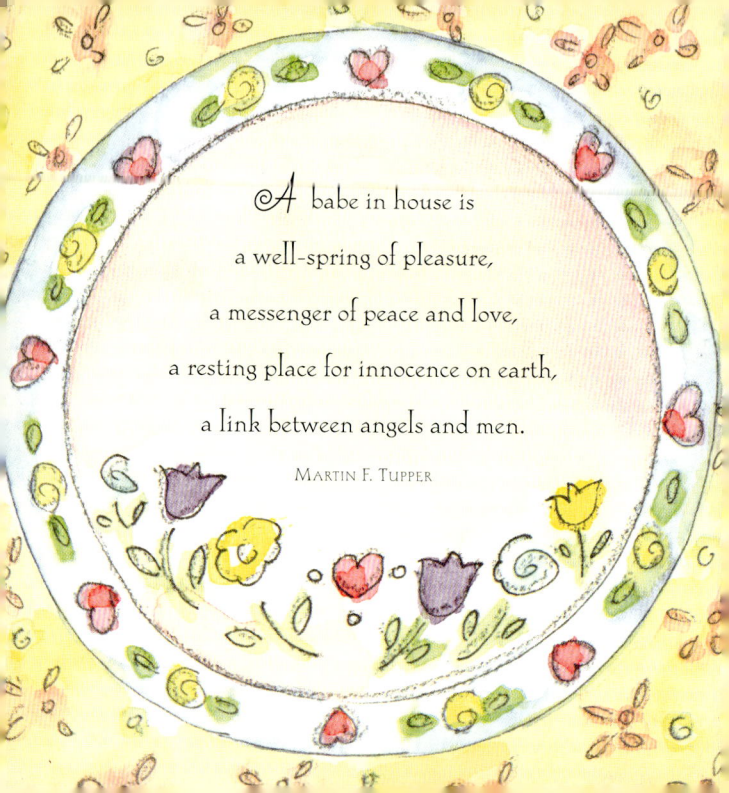

A babe in house is
a well-spring of pleasure,
a messenger of peace and love,
a resting place for innocence on earth,
a link between angels and men.

MARTIN F. TUPPER

Our children are living messages we send to a time and place we will not see.

ANONYMOUS

A baby is God's opinion that the world should go on.

CARL SANDBURG

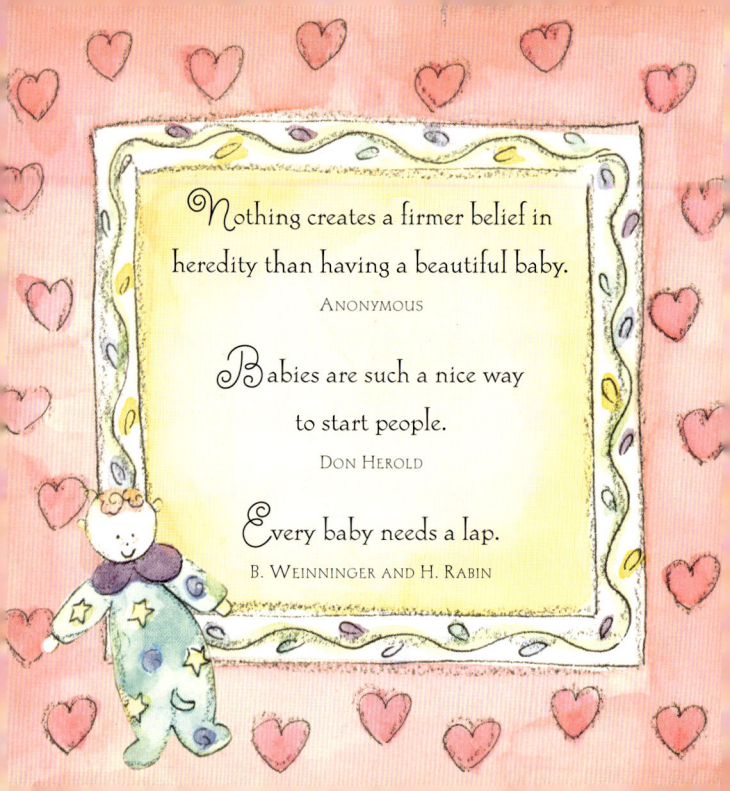

Nothing creates a firmer belief in heredity than having a beautiful baby.

ANONYMOUS

Babies are such a nice way to start people.

DON HEROLD

Every baby needs a lap.

B. WEINNINGER AND H. RABIN

Children need love, especially when they do not deserve it.

HAROLD S. HULBERT

You dear children, are from God.

1 JOHN 4:4

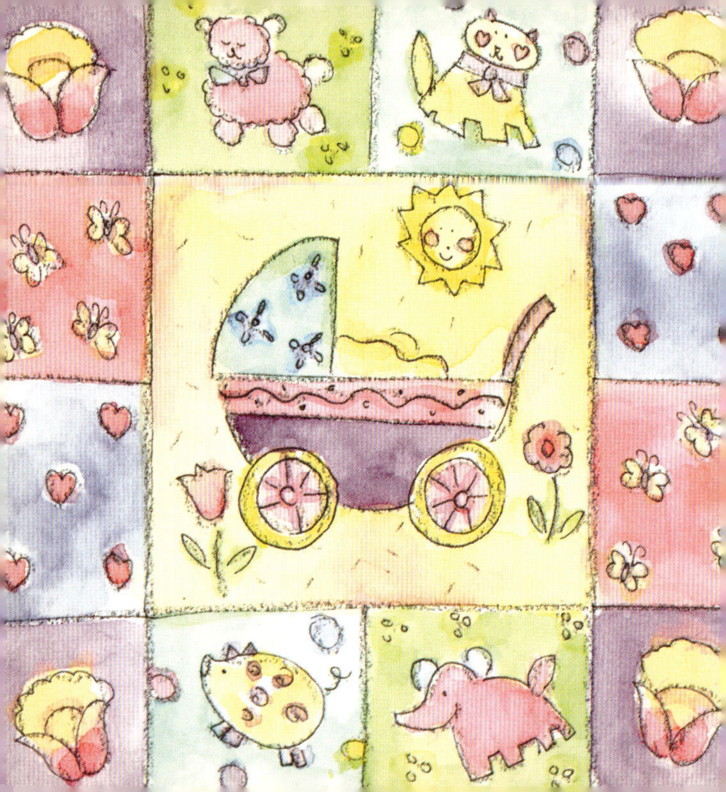

The best thing to spend on your child is your time.

ANONYMOUS

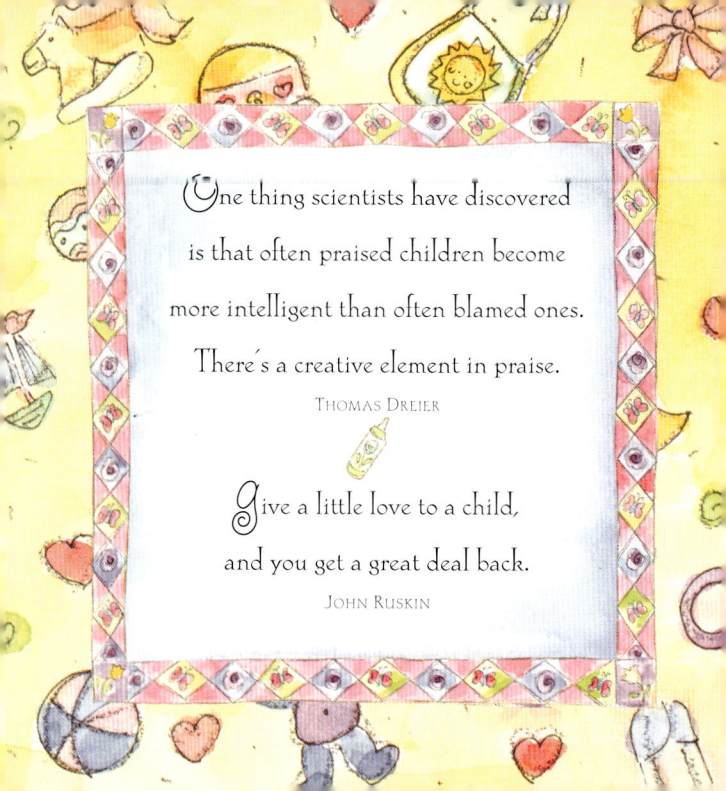

One thing scientists have discovered
is that often praised children become
more intelligent than often blamed ones.
There's a creative element in praise.

THOMAS DREIER

Give a little love to a child,
and you get a great deal back.

JOHN RUSKIN

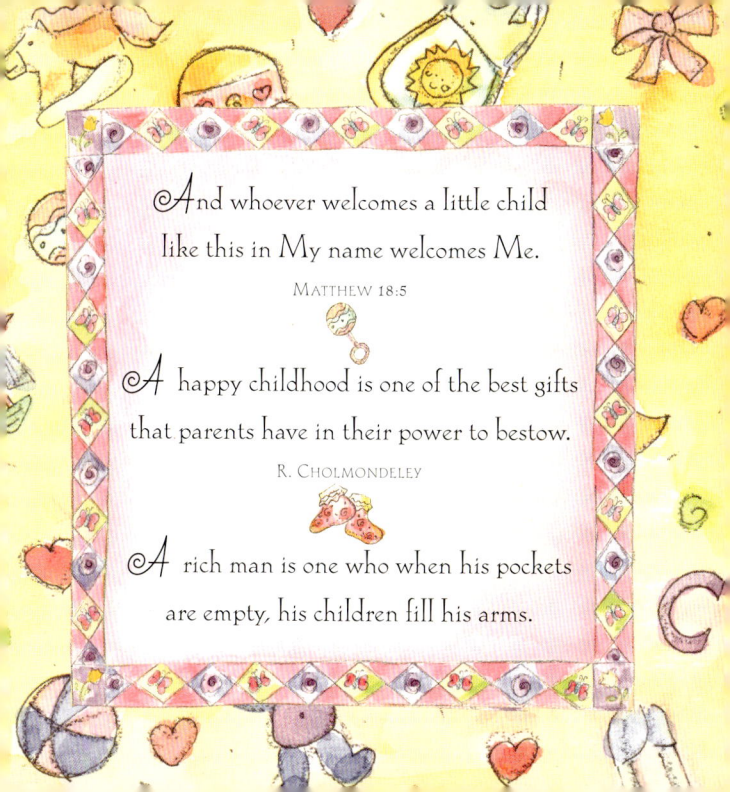

And whoever welcomes a little child
like this in My name welcomes Me.

MATTHEW 18:5

A happy childhood is one of the best gifts
that parents have in their power to bestow.

R. CHOLMONDELEY

A rich man is one who when his pockets
are empty, his children fill his arms.

From the lips of children and infants you have ordained praise.

PSALM 8:2

There are 152 distinctly different ways of holding a baby—and all are right.

HEYWOOD BROUN

Thank Heaven for Little Boys

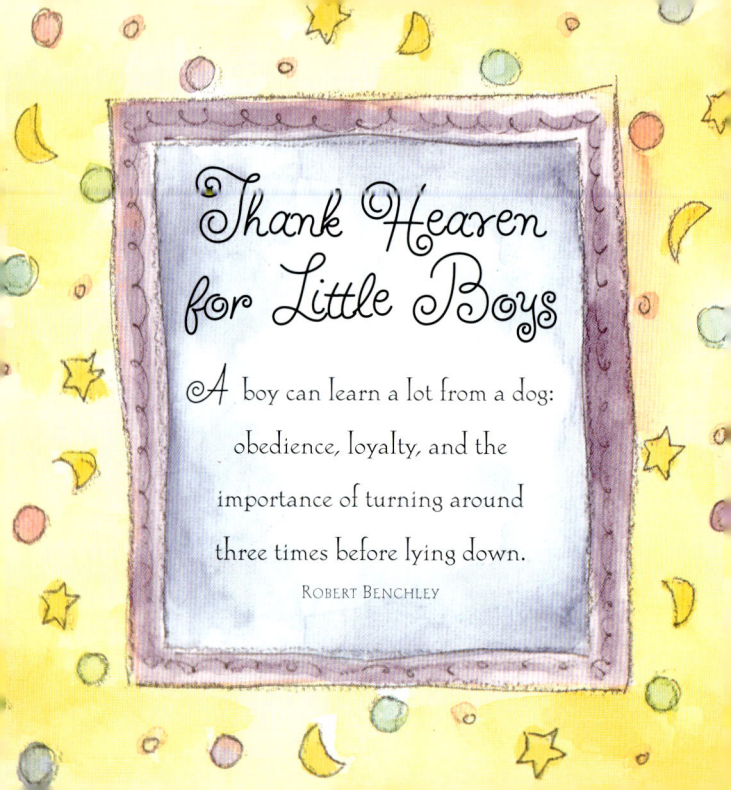

A boy can learn a lot from a dog: obedience, loyalty, and the importance of turning around three times before lying down.

ROBERT BENCHLEY

A baby in your lap may dampen your spirits.

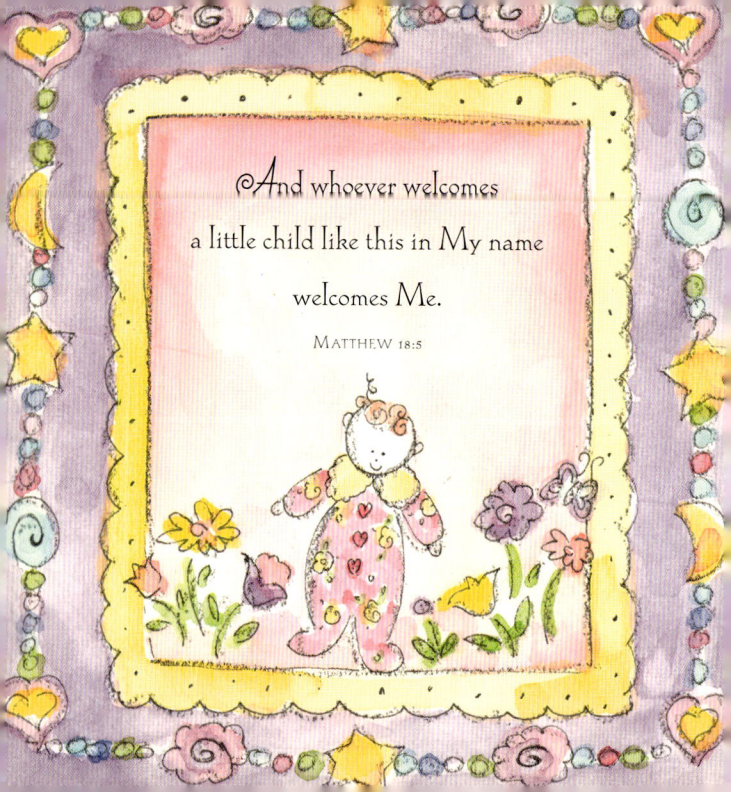

And whoever welcomes a little child like this in My name welcomes Me.

MATTHEW 18:5

Thank Heaven for Little Girls

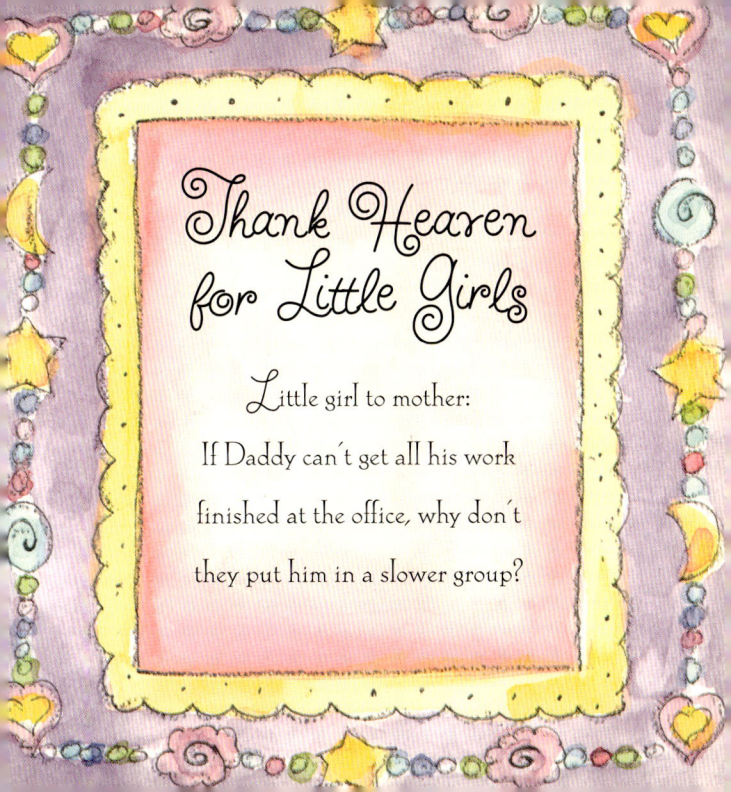

Little girl to mother: If Daddy can't get all his work finished at the office, why don't they put him in a slower group?

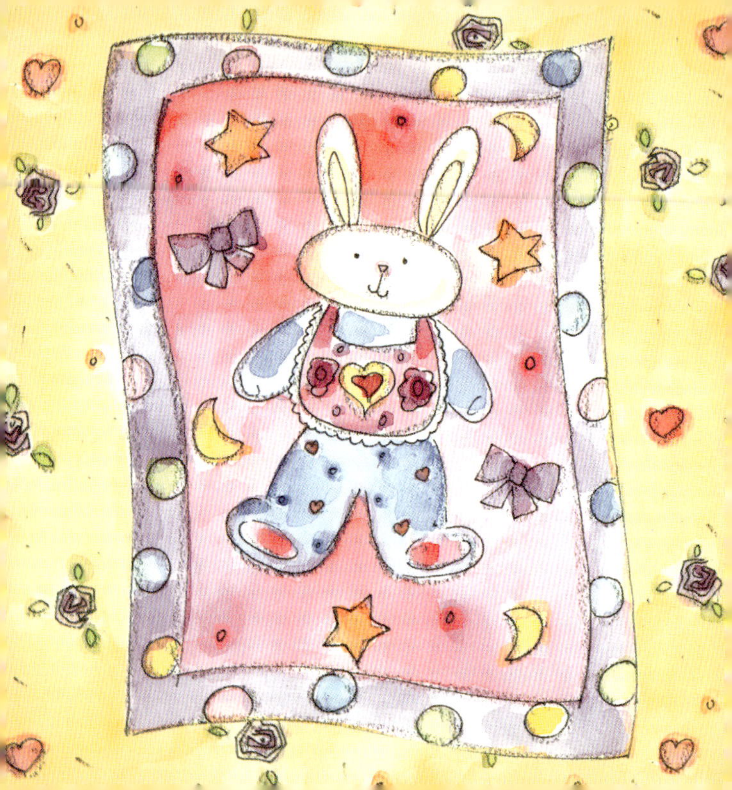

Children Are

Children are God's apostles, sent forth, day by day, to preach of love, and hope and peace.

Children are likely to live up to what you believe in them.

LADY BIRD JOHNSON

Children are a bridge to heaven.

ANCIENT PROVERB

A child does not need to be parented.
He needs to be mothered and fathered.

ZAN THOMPSON

*Y*ou are bone of my bones,
and flesh of my flesh.

GENESIS 2:23

A child reaches for your hand
and touches your heart.

ANONYMOUS

A baby is born with the need
to be loved and never outgrows it.

ANONYMOUS

*H*omes are the building blocks
of civilization.

ARNOLD TOYNBEE

A child brings hope with it
and forward-looking thoughts.

PROVERB

Just like Sponges

Babies are like sponges.

They absorb all your strength and leave you limp.

But give them a squeeze and you get it all back.

ANONYMOUS

Roots and Wings

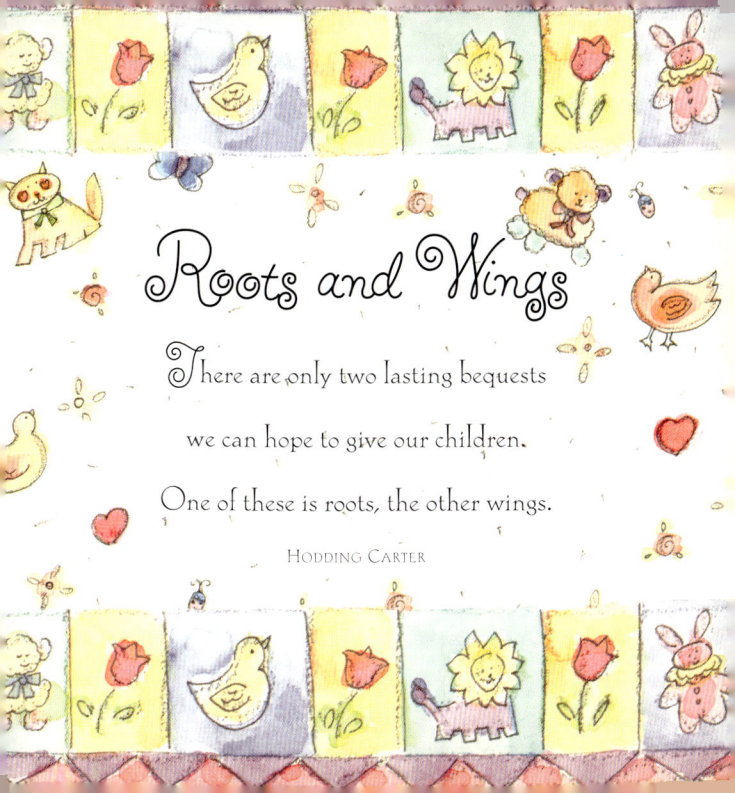

There are only two lasting bequests

we can hope to give our children.

One of these is roots, the other wings.

HODDING CARTER

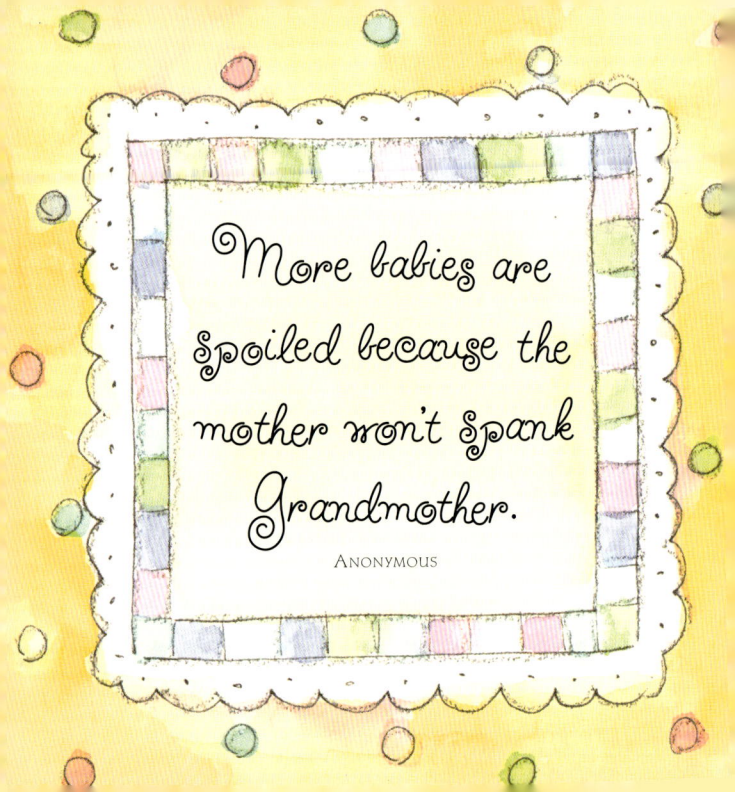

More babies are spoiled because the mother won't spank Grandmother.

ANONYMOUS

Children are the hands by which we take hold of heaven.

HENRY WARD BEECHER

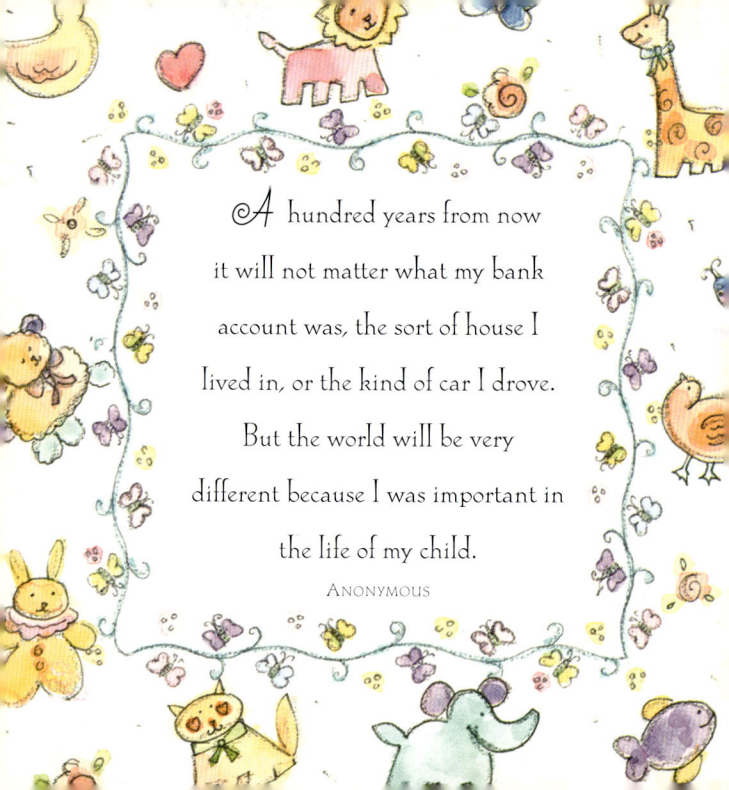

A hundred years from now it will not matter what my bank account was, the sort of house I lived in, or the kind of car I drove. But the world will be very different because I was important in the life of my child.

ANONYMOUS

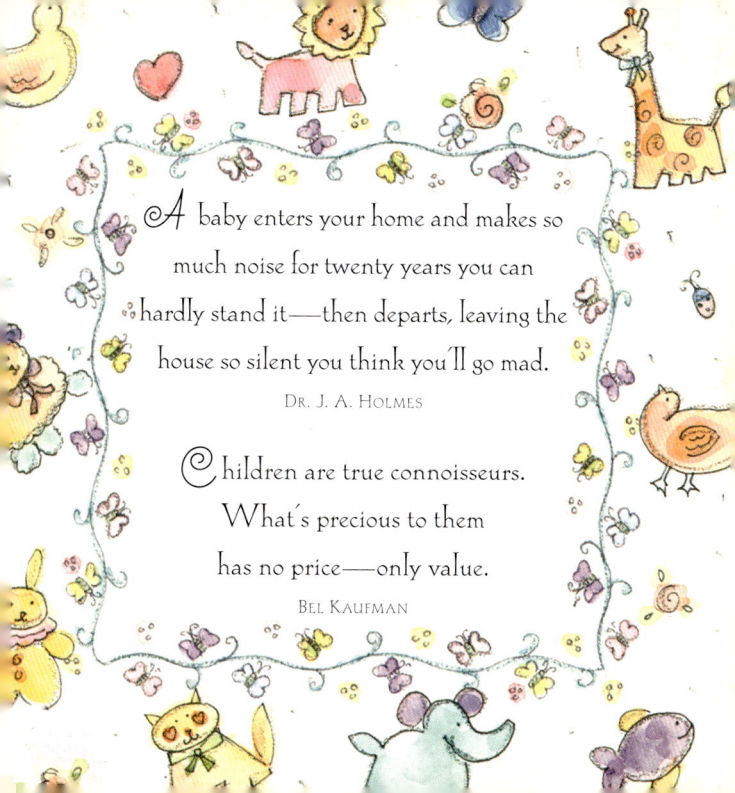

A baby enters your home and makes so much noise for twenty years you can hardly stand it—then departs, leaving the house so silent you think you'll go mad.

Dr. J. A. Holmes

Children are true connoisseurs. What's precious to them has no price—only value.

Bel Kaufman

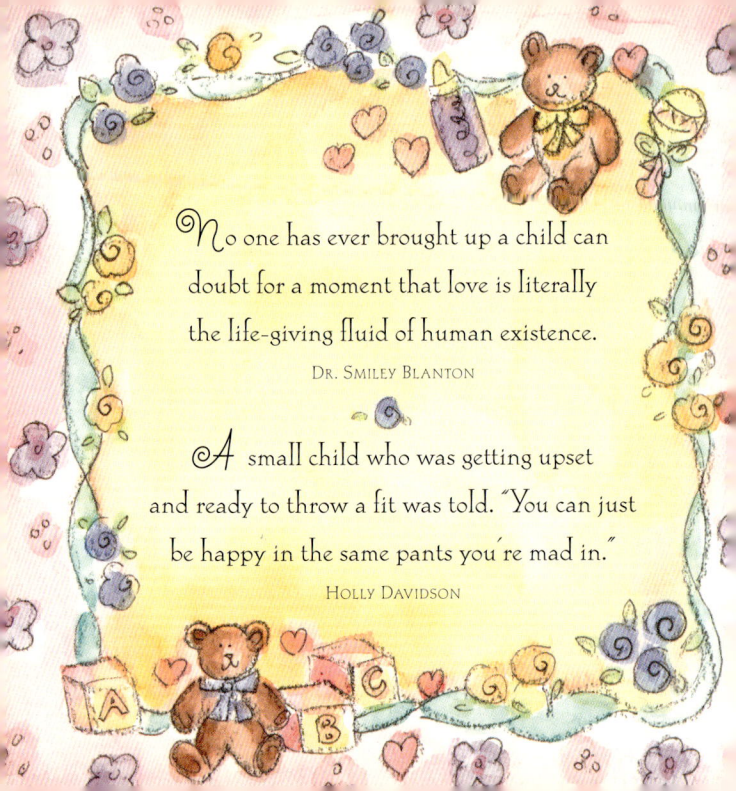

No one has ever brought up a child can doubt for a moment that love is literally the life-giving fluid of human existence.

Dr. Smiley Blanton

A small child who was getting upset and ready to throw a fit was told, "You can just be happy in the same pants you're mad in."

Holly Davidson

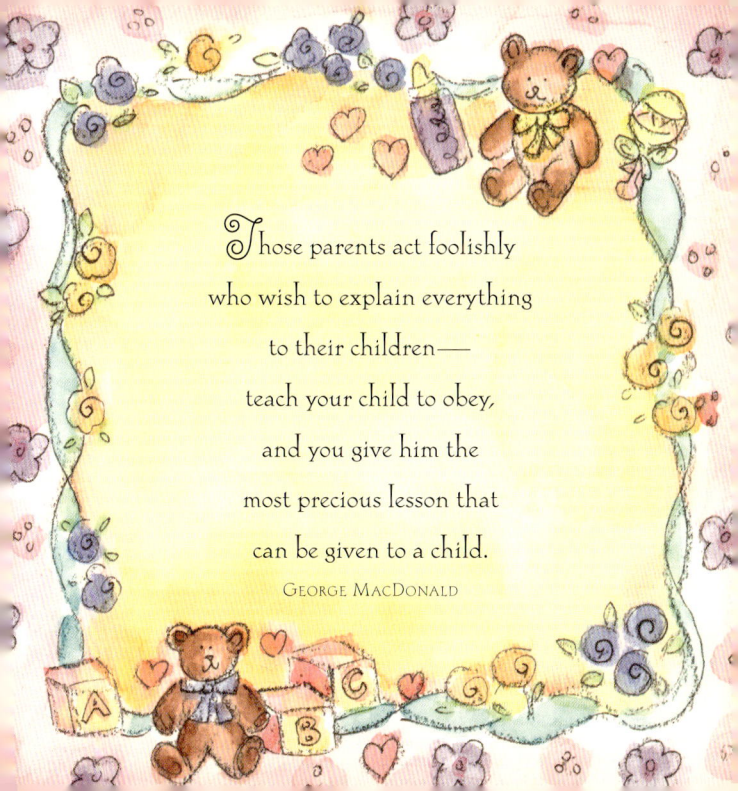

Those parents act foolishly who wish to explain everything to their children— teach your child to obey, and you give him the most precious lesson that can be given to a child.

George MacDonald

As for me and my house, we will serve the Lord.

JOSHUA 24:15

A baby — the most powerful of powerless creatures.

ANONYMOUS

We find delight in the beauty and happiness of children that makes the heart too big for the body.

RALPH WALDO EMERSON

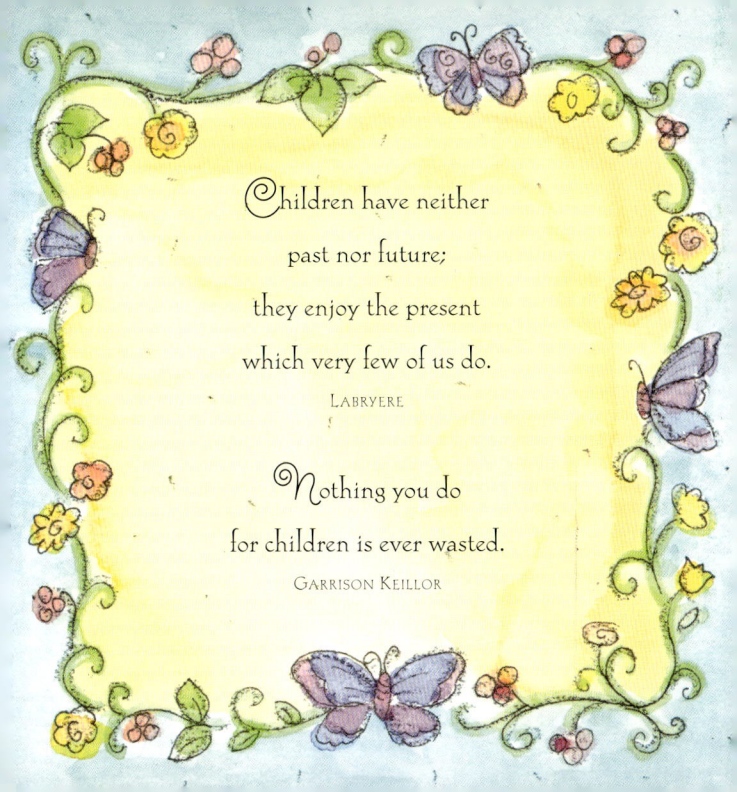

Children have neither past nor future; they enjoy the present which very few of us do.

LABRYERE

Nothing you do for children is ever wasted.

GARRISON KEILLOR

A Grandparent's Love

The importance of grandparents in the life of little children is immeasurable. A young child with the good fortune to have grandparents near by benefits in countless wayst It has a place to share its joys, its sorrows, to find a sympathetic and patient listener, to be loved.

EDWARD WAKIN

There's nothing like a family.

AMERICAN PROVERB

A babe is nothing but

a bundle of possibilities.

HENRY WARD BEECHER

Dear Mom and Dad,

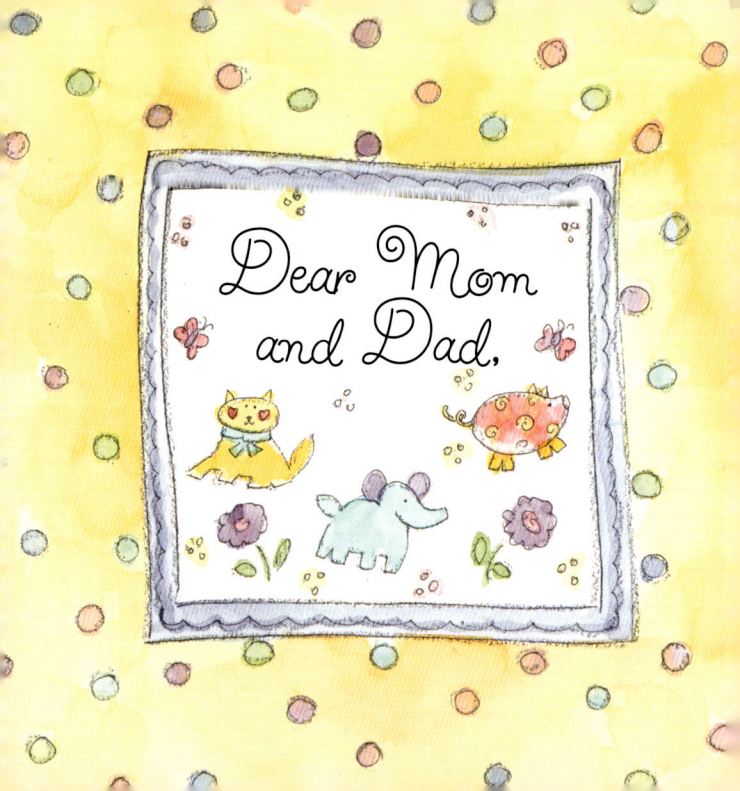

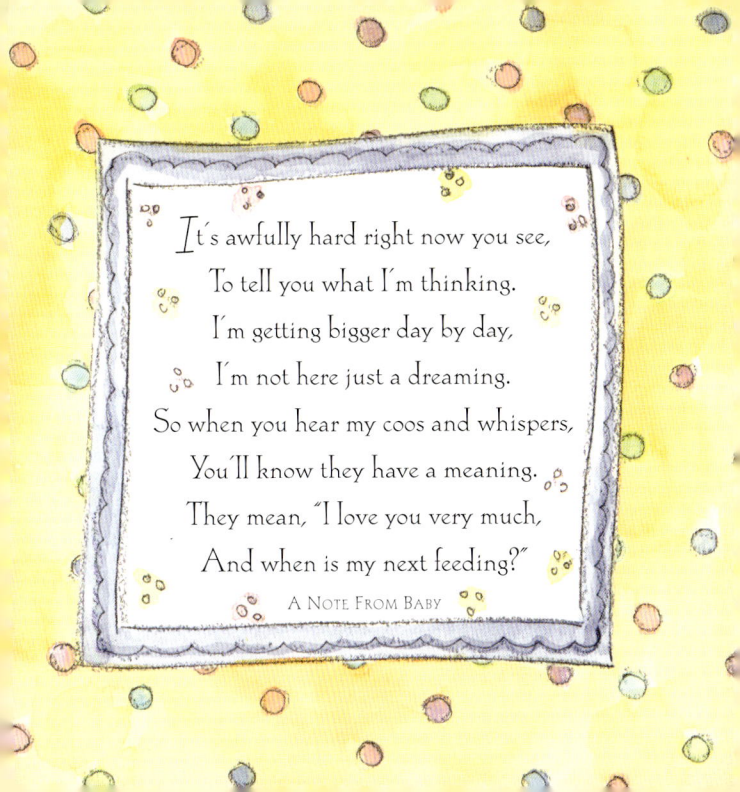

It's awfully hard right now you see,
To tell you what I'm thinking.
I'm getting bigger day by day,
I'm not here just a dreaming.
So when you hear my coos and whispers,
You'll know they have a meaning.
They mean, "I love you very much,
And when is my next feeding?"

A Note From Baby

Life is a flame that is always burning itself out, but it catches fire again every time a baby is born.

GEORGE BERNARD SHAW

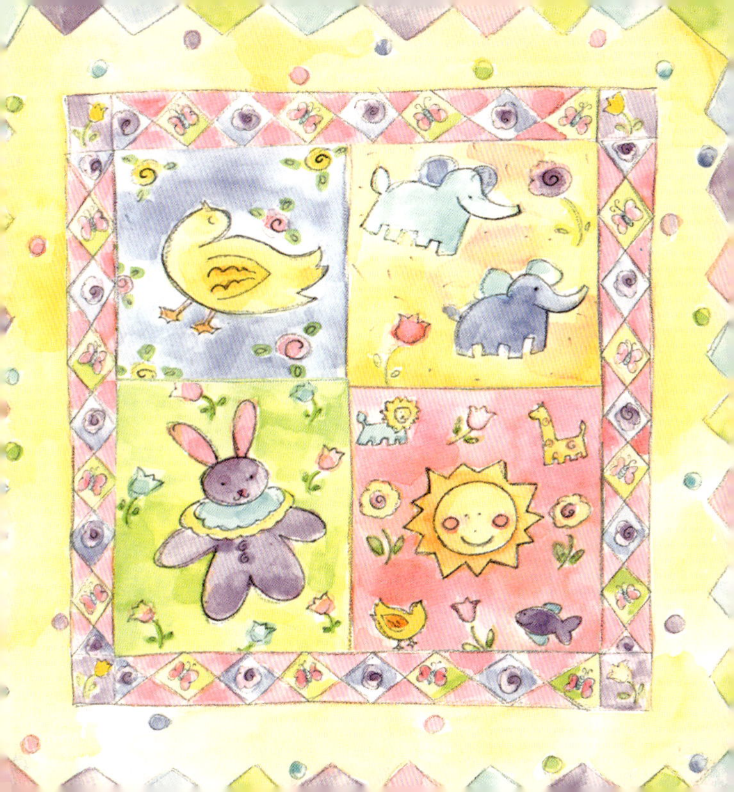

A baby is an inestimable blessing.

MARK TWAIN

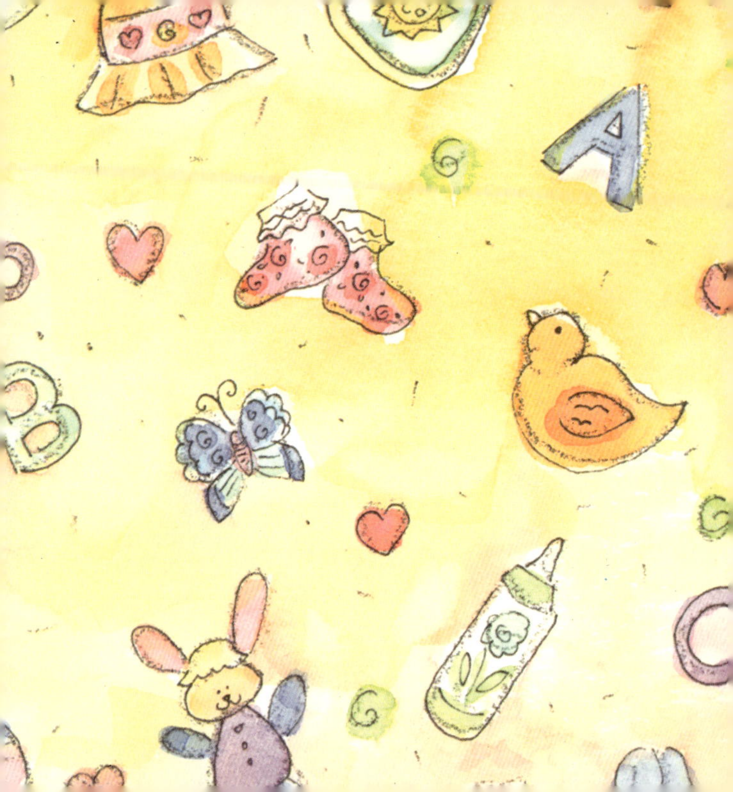